2360

WORLD WAR ONE

1915

Philip J. Haythornthwaite

Front cover illustration: The King's (Liverpool) Regiment await a German attack near Ypres; see plate 23.

Back cover illustration: A French outpost in northern France; see plate 3.

1. The last vestige of colourful uniforms disappeared at the end of 1914 and beginning of 1915. These French light cavalrymen are typical: they wear the light blue tunic with crimson facings, and red breeches with light blue stripe, of the *Chasseurs à Cheval*; they even retain the white trefoil epaulettes. The kepi insignia appear to identify them as members of the 11th Regt; note the 'tent-hat'-style forage-caps of two of the seated figures. The man in the background wears a trophy *Pickelhaube*, which appears to bear the winged lion badge of Baden. The sign on this railway boxcar, 'Hommes 36-40, Chevaux 8' (36–40 men or 8 horses) was one remarked upon with disdain by countless Allied soldiers of all nations who served on the Western Front.

▼ 1

WORLD WAR ONE: 1915

Philip J. Haythornthwaite

ARMS AND
ARMOUR

2. One of the first casualties of the war was the traditional French uniform of dark blue coat and red trousers, supplanted from late 1914 by the uniform illustrated, in a colour styled 'horizon blue' or 'tricolor grey', the latter description arising from its manufacture from interwoven strands of red, white and blue. The resulting lightish grey-blue shade proved to be an adequate camouflage and was retained throughout the war. The cut of the uniform remained basically the same (a tunic with standing collar and a double-breasted greatcoat for infantry), although a common variation was a single-breasted greatcoat for cavalry and a similar pattern for infantry but with breast-pockets. The red kepi had been equipped with grey-blue covers from the outbreak of war, and was now produced in 'horizon blue', retaining its black leather peak. Equipment remained of black leather.

◀**2**

INTRODUCTION

First published in Great Britain in 1989 by Arms and Armour Press, Artillery House, Artillery Row, London SW1P 1RT.

Distributed in the USA by Sterling Publishing Co. Inc., 387 Park Avenue South, New York, NY 10016-8810, USA.

Distributed in Australia by Capricorn Link (Australia) Pty. Ltd., P.O. Box 665, Lane Cove, New South Wales 2066, Australia.

British Library Cataloguing in Publication Data:
Haythornthwaite, Philip J. (Philip John), 1951–
World War One: 1915. — (soldiers fotofax)
1. World War 1
I. Title II. Series
940.3
ISBN 1-85409-005-4

Designed and edited by DAG Publications Ltd. Designed by David Gibbons; layout by Cilla Eurich; typeset by Ronset Typesetters Ltd, Darwen Lancashire, and by Typesetters (Birmingham) Limited, Warley, West Midlands; camerawork by M&E Reproductions, North Fambridge, Essex; printed and bound in Great Britain by The Alden Press Limited, Oxford.

It might be argued that 1915 was the year in which the realities of World War became obvious. The experience on the two major fronts that had been opened in 1914 proved that the war would not be 'over by Christmas' as many had predicted; that neither France nor Russia would be defeated by rapid German advances; nor would Germany be overcome easily by the Allies.

1915 began in virtual stalemate on both Eastern and Western Fronts, and when the year ended, despite considerable German gains on the Eastern Front and a terrible effusion of blood and casualties on a scale undreamed of in earlier wars, this stalemate persisted. Moreover, the war had widened considerably with the entry of Turkey on the side of the Central Powers (she had become involved in 1914, but the real, full-scale combat began only in 1915) and the opening of a new front when Italy joined the Allies.

However, perhaps the most significant features of 1915 were those aspects of the war which raised the combat to a new level of 'frightfulness' (to use a word that featured large in the vocabulary of contemporary Press reports when describing the conduct of the enemy!) – the expedition to the Dardanelles and the use of gas. Although the former established the reputation of the ANZAC soldier for posterity, it produced conditions so terrible that the very geographical term 'Gallipoli' is sufficient to epitomise appalling privation, mismanagement and the most bitter combat. The use of poison gas – initially on the Eastern Front but most effectively in the West from April 1915 – introduced yet another level of horror into the war. Initially condemned by the Allies, toxic gas was ultimately adopted by them so that both armies were compelled to wear masks, which rendered them as unearthly in appearance as the nature of the war itself. In uniforms and equipment, 1915 saw the increasing use of camouflage, with the abandonment of the red and blue French uniform and its replacement by 'horizon blue' and, in a fashion at once archaic but necessary, the emergence of steel 'shrapnel helmets', pioneered by France.

Many thousands of photographs were published at the time in contemporary works and periodicals (for example, the *Illustrated War News*, *Navy & Army Illustrated*, *Sphere* and *Illustrated London News* in Britain, from which some of the images here have been taken), but contemporary captions should be viewed with circumspection. Trenches that are pristine, with immaculately-uniformed occupants, are almost certainly not scenes from the front no matter what the caption may say, while others purporting to be views of the war are not: in many cases these are obvious (such as that depicting 'Infantery laring cower' [sic] illustrated here), but in other cases it is difficult to determine the authenticity.

Throughout this series it is intended that the central data section should provide a chronology of the year in question and detail the arms and equipment of the main combatants; in this case the concentration is upon the British Army.

▲3

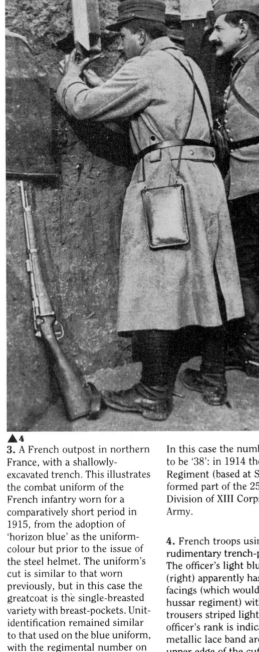

▲4

3. A French outpost in northern France, with a shallowly-excavated trench. This illustrates the combat uniform of the French infantry worn for a comparatively short period in 1915, from the adoption of 'horizon blue' as the uniform-colour but prior to the issue of the steel helmet. The uniform's cut is similar to that worn previously, but in this case the greatcoat is the single-breasted variety with breast-pockets. Unit-identification remained similar to that used on the blue uniform, with the regimental number on the collar-patches of the tunic and greatcoat, initially intended to be in a distinctive 'branch' colour – yellow with blue numeral for infantry – but soon the patch reverted to the shade of the garment with only the number in a contrasting colour.

In this case the number appears to be '38': in 1914 the 38th Regiment (based at St-Etienne) formed part of the 25th Infantry Division of XIII Corps in First Army.

4. French troops using a rudimentary trench-periscope. The officer's light blue tunic (right) apparently has light blue facings (which would indicate a hussar regiment) with red trousers striped light blue. The officer's rank is indicated by the metallic lace band around the upper edge of the cuff and the chevron on the front of the forage-cap. The extreme neatness of the trench and smartness of the uniforms indicate that this photograph depicts a demonstration trench rather than one in the front line; nevertheless, such images are of

◀5

6 ▲

7 ▲

great value in illustrating the minutiae of equipment and the theoretical construction of trenches. The rifle is the 1892-pattern carbine.

5. Contrasting with some immaculate 'trench' photographs taken behind the lines, this group of dishevelled French infantry has a greater air of authenticity. These *poilus* (also styled *piou-piou*!) enjoy a meal and a smoke under the 'protection' of a chicken-wire trench roof. This was intended to prevent the entry of grenades into the trench; if these were thrown they would not explode at the level of the trench floor but would still cause considerable damage. The men here appear to wear the new 'horizon blue', but at least two patterns of greatcoat are shown, double- and single-breasted.

6. Also in contrast to the muddy trenches usually associated with the Western Front were the lines in the hilly terrain of the Vosges, such as this defence-work manned by French *Chasseurs Alpins*. They exhibit the usual mixture of regulation and other dress, mufflers and leather jerkins being added to the dark blue tunic and floppy beret which characterized the French mountain troops (infantry and artillery) and from which they took their nickname of 'blue devils'. This trench is topped by a parapet of dry-stone walling with loopholes through which to fire, with the ubiquitous barbed wire entanglement in front.

7. The field uniform of the German Army began to be modified in 1915; the distinctive buttoned cuffs were replaced by a simple, turned-back cuff, and

the piping was removed from the rear vents. In September 1915 a new tunic was authorized, the *Bluse*, in which the breast-buttons were concealed by a fly-front, but the previous patterns were still worn for some considerable time. This uniform includes the 1910-pattern field-grey tunic with 'Saxon' cuffs and 1909-pattern leather equipment; the *Pickelhaube* has a detachable

cover and the spike removed; and note the rolled-up shoulder-straps. The original of this photograph is captioned on the reverse by a British soldier, 'Not a bad looking lad for a Boche', and states that he had a number of photographs 'on him'; it was thus taken from the subject either as a prisoner or from his dead body.

▲8 ▼9

▼10

8. The German Army was a composite force of the troops of the various states, which to a degree retained their identity within the overall organization. In this photograph the King of Saxony inspects a detachment of Saxon troops; their identity is not completely clear from the picture, but the *Pickelhaube*-cover of one man appears to bear the number 104, which would indicate the 5th Saxon Regt. (Crown Prince's), which in 1914 was the senior infantry unit in the XIX (Saxon) Corps. It is interesting to observe the use of the 18th-century practice of troops following the reviewing dignitary with their eyes during the inspection, retained by some nations to the present day.

9. Among modifications to the German field uniform were those made to the *Pickelhaube*. It was made with a removable spike or ball, and cloth covers were produced with no accommodation for the spike; a number of cheaper (*Ersatz*) patterns were produced, helmets made of pressed steel (painted black or field-grey), pressed felt or even *papier mâché*, with mounts of thin, dull grey metal. Another variety rarely illustrated is that shown here, of field-grey felt with a small ventilation-knob on the top, without ornaments save in some cases a small plaque on the front bearing the unit-number. This headdress could be worn with a neck-curtain, and was worn thus in Serbia; similar neck-covers could be used in any hot climate, like Macedonia. The tunic here is similar to the amended 1915 pattern but with standing collar.

10. German troops marching-past in Lille. The mounted officer and at least one of the column appear to have the three-button 'Brandenburg' cuff, while others seem to have the modified 'turned back' cuff, the amendment of the original field-grey service uniform prior to the devising of the 1915 *Bluse*.

11. A German machine-gun mounted for use in an anti-aircraft role. The gun is the Model 1908 *Maschinengewehr*; the tube that leads from near the muzzle carried the water-coolant for the water-jacket or *Mantel*, which surrounded the barrel to prevent over-heating. This photograph shows how the 'sleigh' mounting could be adjusted to position the gun as required; also shown clearly is the erect rear sight. The regimental identity of the crew is not clear, but they wear the 1910-pattern tunic with 'Brandenburg' cuff; and note the coloured knot attached to the bayonet of the man at extreme right, which identified battalion and company.

12. A German machine-gun unit wearing the shako with cloth field cover used by the Jägers and machine-gun units. Their Maxim guns have the wheeled 'sleigh' mounting; the team in the foreground demonstrates how it could be fired from a prone position. Metal protective shields measuring 97 x 80cm, painted khaki, could be fitted to infantry Maxims, the gunner having to sight his target through a hole in the shield, restricting his field of vision though gaining protection from enemy fire. A further disadvantage was the fact that the shield disrupted camouflage, so that in Austrian service it was usual to throw a khaki-green or olive cloth over the shield to break up its hard edges.

▲13

13. Submachine-guns were not in common use during the war, but an automatic rifle was used by the German Army in small numbers. Three units styled *Musketen-Bataillone* were created in mid-1915, composed of four-man sections crewing one automatic rifle (30 rifles per company, 90 per battalion; company-establishment was 4 officers and 160 other ranks). The *Muskete* had a length of 44in

▼14

and a 25-round magazine; it was similar to the Danish Madsen automatic rifle and had a bipod mounting. It was used principally as a defensive weapon, its crews being positioned behind the front line to oppose any breakthrough.

14. A column of German infantry marching up to the front line on the Western Front. A number of interesting items are visible

here, notably the waterproof trousers (reasonably common by this date) and the bandoliers of extra ammunition hung around the neck. A further attempt to exclude the Flanders mud is the presence of extensive wrappings around the breeches and mechanisms of the rifles, clearly visible on the central man of the second rank. The use of the undress cap even in combat zones was widespread.

15. Men of the 1st Battalion Royal Scots Fusiliers manning a defensive position made from a ruined house and sandbags, at St-Eloi, south of Ypres, in about April or May 1915. The battalion landed in France in August 1914 as part of the 3rd Division; in early April it transferred from the 9th Brigade to the 8th, but remained in the 3rd Division throughout the war. The appearance of the men here is

15 ▲

16 ▲   17 ▼

absolutely typical of British infantry at this time, plus the regimental glengarry cap; note the covers around the mechanism of the Lee-Enfield rifle to exclude mud and dust.

16. The officers' uniform of the British Army is splendidly illustrated in this photograph of Major C. W. Hines of the 7th Battalion Durham Light Infantry. The khaki uniform has bronzed badges, the cap- and collar-insignia consisting of a crowned bugle-horn with 'DLI' in the centre, and on the collar the letter 'T' beneath, signifying 'Territorial'. The 7th Battalion was based at Sunderland, landed at Boulogne in April, and was in the Northumbrian Division (later 151st Brigade, 50th Dvision). The inscription on the original records that Major Hines survived barely five weeks after landing.

17. Britain had used the Maxim as its principal machine-gun, but the Vickers gun, which came into widespread use in 1915, became the standard weapon and was so efficient and reliable that (in successive modifications) it remained in use until well after the Second World War. Firing a .303in bullet at a rate of between 450 and 500 rounds per minute, it was a water-cooled weapon into which cartridges were fed on a fabric belt, into the slot clearly visible just to the rear of the water-jacket in this photograph. Its tripod mounting enabled it to be used in an anti-aircraft role, as here, without modification. The gunners appear to wear the grey kilts of the London Scottish.

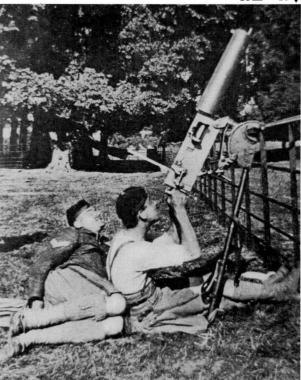

▲18

18. A private of the Black Watch in field equipment, illustrating the camouflaged khaki apron worn over the kilt, puttees over the hose, and the 1914-pattern equipment introduced from late 1914 or early 1915 to compensate for shortages of the 1908-pattern web equipment. It was intended that the 1914-pattern (which copied the 1908 but in brown leather, save for pouch-type cartridge-carriers) should be reserved for units training at home, but before long it was used on active service. An unusual feature here is the waterproof rain-hat; it is conceivable that the dark triangle on the front is some form of company- or battalion-identification.

19. In an attempt to overcome the effects of waterlogged trenches, various expedients were utilized ranging from 'gum-boots' to waders. Illustrated here

▲19

is a member of the 3/3rd Battalion City of London Regiment (Royal Fusiliers) wearing the 'wader-stockings' designed by F. B. Behr and pronounced a most effective method of remaining dry-shod even in freezing water. The waterproof waders were lined with wool and worn over the bare feet (i.e., without socks), inside the boots; damage could be repaired with a bicycle-tyre repair-kit. The battalion shown was raised in January 1915 and remained in Britain until late in the war, when it was absorbed by the 3rd Battalion. The 1914-pattern leather equipment is shown clearly; and the rank-insignia of a crown over three chevrons was that of company sergeant-major and company quartermaster-sergeant until 1915, and CQMS thereafter.

20. The different duties required by active service resulted in many variations in uniform. This private wears a costume unusual for his regiment, the Argyll and Sutherland Highlanders: riding-breeches and leather gaiters as worn by personnel of the regimental transport, instead of the usual kilt and hose. His tunic is the standard pattern, not the 'doublet' with cut-back skirts which distinguished Highland regiments; and the headdress is the balmoral-style bonnet introduced to replace the unfunctional glengarry in 1915. Known as a 'Tam O'Shanter', the bonnet was initially issued in blue cloth with khaki cover, and later made of khaki cloth; instead of the large cap-badges many units wore less-obtrusive tartan patches in the field.

21. Most of Belgium was overrun in 1914, and the remaining Belgian forces were dependent upon Britain and France for their uniforms and equipment. From early 1915 a khaki uniform was adopted, largely because the material was available from Britain; thus it resembled the British pattern but had leather gaiters instead of puttees. The new equipment was brown leather, and coloured collar-patches were worn on the tunic. Later the appearance became more French after the adoption of the Adrian helmet, painted khaki to match the uniform-colour.

20 ▲   21 ▼

▲22 ▼23 ▼24

25. Trench-warfare led to the reintroduction of the hand-grenade, a weapon that had enjoyed a considerable reputation in the late 17th century. Among the earliest grenades were simple iron spheres filled with combustible material ignited by tugging the fuze as they were thrown; this French infantryman demonstrates how a leather wrist-loop was utilized to ensure that ignition occurred as the grenade was thrown. Farther down the trench is a man who appears to be equipped with a rifle-grenade.

26. New types of artillery were devised for close support of the infantry in trench warfare; the trench-mortar was the principal development. In French service, weapons of great age were re-utilized to lob projectiles with high-angle fire into the enemy trenches, mortars as ancient as the 1830s being used until the development in 1915 of the first purpose-built weapon, the Mortar '58 cal. No 1', followed by other patterns. An odd development at this time was the 'aerial torpedo', a projectile resembling a conventional mortar-bomb with large fins to provide stability in flight. Recoil of the launch was absorbed by the large base-plate depicted here.

26 ▼

25 ▲

22. Contemporary captions should always be viewed with a degree of circumspection: views purporting to have been photographed on active service were sometimes staged for home consumption. This is included here as perhaps the most glaring example, published in France in 1915 supposedly depicting *Infanterie anglaise en ambuscade* and by implication at the front; actually it appears to depict a cadet unit on exercise at home. The 'English' caption which accompanied the French publication, "Infantry laring cower", did little to elucidate!

23. This photograph – remarkable if it is what it purports to be – was published in June 1915 and shows a German attack upon a position held by The King's (Liverpool) Regiment near Ypres. As the British wait with fixed bayonets, an officer crouches in mid-ground ready to direct his men. The caps worn here are the ordinary service variety with wire-stiffened crown; it was common on active service to wear a softer cap, without the stiffening, known as a 'trench cap'.

24. A French machine-gun post at Neuville St-Vaast, established in a shallow trench. The gun appears to be the Model 1907, known as the St-Etienne (from its being designed at the National Arms Factory there), a development of the Model 1905 (Puteaux, similarly named from the place of development). It was air-cooled and could achieve a rate of fire of up to 650 rounds per minute (normally 500). Ammunition was in the form of 'racks' of 25 rounds, the comb-like objects visible in the illustration, being handed from the ammunition-box at the foot of the trench. Two of the gunners have anti-gas goggles around their kepis.

▲27 ▼28

▲29

31. From about July 1915 the French Army assumed the appearance it held for the remainder of the war, with the adoption of the 'casque Adrian', the steel shrapnel-helmet with medial ridge and front and rear peaks. Named after its designer, it was copied from the helmets of French firemen and was painted to match the uniform-colour. On the front it bore a stamped metal badge: a grenade for infantry and cavalry; grenade and crossed cannon-barrels for artillery; horn for light infantry; grenade and anchor for marines; helmet and corselet for engineers; and a crescent for Moroccans; all with the letters 'RF' (*République Française*). Stars were affixed to the front for general officers. These infantrymen wear typical service uniform with the helmet, and the 1915 single-breasted greatcoat with breast-pockets; the man on the right has in addition to his ordinary equipment a small automatic pistol tucked behind his shoulder-belt, and apparently a dagger, both of use in close-quarter fighting in the trenches.

31 ▼

27. A number of ancient armaments re-appeared in the First World War, most notably the steel helmet, but more bizarre was this contraption, a crossbow manufactured for the projection of hand-grenades. *L'Arbalète Lance-Grenade*, known colloquially as a 'grasshopper', was used by the French Army to hurl bombs a distance of between 20 and 80 metres. This particular example has a shaped stock like a rifle, the propulsion power arising from the steel and wire construction.

28. A popular method of manufacturing anti-aircraft protection was to affix a machine-gun to a wagon-wheel upon a post, the wheel parallel to the ground. This German construction takes the principle a stage further by mounting a field-gun upon a beehive-shaped wooden platform, which allowed it to traverse to follow the enemy aircraft. The gun appears to be the 1896-pattern 77mm *Feld Kanone*. The crew's protective dug-out is quite sophisticated and sturdily-built.

29. With sniping a common danger of trench-warfare, numerous patterns of periscope were devised to allow observation without danger, some sophisticated and others extremely rudimentary. One of the former is illustrated here, disguised with sacking and grass where it protrudes over the parapet. The viewer is apparently a German *Unteroffizier*, his rank indicated by the broad lace on the collar, but the identity of the unit is not evident from his shoulder-strap.

30. The first steel helmet of the war was a skull-cap without a brim used by the French Army, worn under the kepi or, as here, on top of it, giving the appearance of a peaked crash-helmet. It could be worn without the kepi (a very medieval appearance), and was painted light grey-blue to match the uniforms. The appearance of the classic 'casque Adrian' from mid-1915 replaced the skull-cap, though the earlier pattern was apparently quite effective: when the *Illustrated London News* published this photograph it reported an analysis of head-wounds on 42 men without the cap (23 severe or fatal) and on 13 who wore it, only 5 of whom suffered superficial injury. Note that one of the infantrymen here retains the earlier blue greatcoat.

30 ▲

▲ 32   ▼ 33

32. Armoured cars were common in many armies, the majority providing the crew with more protection than this French example. Cars mounted with machine-guns originated in the French Army with Captain Genty's *auto-mitrailleuse* of 1905–6, basically a Hotchkiss gun affixed to the back of his 1904 Panhard & Levassor automobile. Genty demonstrated the value of such vehicles in North African campaigning. According to its French identification, this photograph of a car firing over a street-barricade was taken in action; shortly after this a shell hit the ruined building to the left of the barricade, killing the NCO firing the gun and injuring the loader.

33. French casualty-evacuation in the Argonne. Supposedly a genuine photograph rather than one posed for the photographer, this shows French troops clearing casualties, a task never solely the responsibility of the official medical personnel. Stretchers are not used here: one casualty is being carried in a blanket. Note the anti-gas goggles worn around the kepi; the small pouch worn on a strap around the neck would contain the anti-gas face-mask.

34. A British casualty, with a bandaged lower right leg and liberally smeared with Flanders mud, is loaded into an ambulance by German medical personnel. This shows the peaked cap worn by transport and medical units of the German Army; in field-grey, it had a blue band piped red for medical staff. The rectangular box suspended from the second button of the tunic of the orderly immediately behind the bandaged leg is a battery-operated flashlight. Note the white brassards with red cross worn on the left upper arm, the universal symbol of medical personnel in many armies.

35. The introduction of distinctive battalion-insignia into the British Army occurred from early 1915; it only really proliferated in later years. A common location of this insignia was at the bottom of the collar at the rear, where they could be identified by following troops in action. The officer here is unidentified, but the badge appears to resemble the red felt Prince of Wales's plumes worn by the 1st Battalion The Welsh Regiment.

36. Family groups of this type are among the most common

34 ▲

images from the First World War (for all nations) yet can illustrate most interesting items of uniform and equipment. This member of the Lancashire Fusiliers wears the spurred boots and cavalry bandolier of the regimental transport, and the soft 'trench cap' with stiffening removed, colloquially termed a 'Gorblimey'. The sleeve-insignia is the white '8' on a red diamond worn by the 1/8th Battalion, a unit based in Salford and which served at Gallipoli.

35 ▼

36 ▼

37. ▲37 ▼38

37. This bizarre photograph illustrates a group of German prisoners captured by the French near Bois le Prêtre, according to the original caption. The diminutive prisoner being questioned by the large, caped French officer measured 4ft 9in; but to illustrate such a 'Puny Hun' (sic) could be counter-productive for propaganda purposes, so the *Illustrated War News* accompanied the photograph with an account of how fit and strong the ordinary German prisoner was, thus explaining why the Allies were not immediately victorious over undersized recruits of this stature, wearing an over-large 1910-pattern tunic.

38. This photograph was published in 1915 as having been taken by a Russian aviator, showing a German advance on the Eastern Front preceded by a barrage of poison gas. Later in the war this terrible weapon was delivered by shells (especially effective when 'mustard gas' was used, as this dreadful concoction did not require employment in dense clouds to be fully effective); but initially the method of delivery utilized the strength of the wind to blow it towards the enemy. Cylinders of toxic gas might be buried with pipes leading out into no-man's-land, to be released in a cloud when the wind-direction was appropriate, as here. Infantry would second the attack, but unless equipped with respirators, they were vulnerable to a shift in wind direction.

39. Many varieties of protective masks were utilized in the period of the early use of poison gas, ranging from simple pads taped over the mouth to hoods covering the entire head. This French device is one devised in 1915 by Dr Detourbe: a wire grille worn over the nose and mouth with a similar grille attached by a hinge at the bridge of the nose, with a pad of impregnated cotton-wool fitted between the two. With such contraptions the French Army frequently wore goggles to protect the eyes.

39 ▲

40. At the date of this photograph only the Germans used poison gas, yet their troops were equally vulnerable if the gas-clouds blew towards them. Protection at this stage was no more sophisticated than a chemically impregnated pad worn over the mouth, but for resuscitation medical orderlies were equipped with oxygen-bottles carried on a breast-harness, with flexible tube and face-mask to treat the partially asphixiated. This is apparently Grenadier Regiment No. 12 (2nd Brandenburg, Prince Carl of Prussia), which in 1914 formed part of III Corps. The stretcher shown has a hinged end, which allowed the casualty's head to be raised.

41. A Highlander wearing an early variety of anti-gas protection, resembling a veil plus goggles; which, as one contemporary caption to this photograph remarked, resembled the Sphinx. The photograph also illustrates the khaki apron with pocket which could be worn over the kilt as an aid to camouflage; these were

introduced as early as the Boer War but were not especially popular, and photographs also show the kilt worn without the apron. The puttees are worn over the hose.

40 ▼   41 ▲

CHRONOLOGY: 1915

1914 ended with action in four principal theatres. On the Western Front, the fluid manoeuvre of the first campaigns had ended with the establishment of trench-lines running from the North Sea to Switzerland; the virtual stalemate of the next four years was established. On the Eastern Front, stalemate also existed, with Russia and Serbia holding the Austro-Germans in check. Turkey's entry into the war on the side of the Central Powers put additional pressure upon Russia, which was already considerably dependent upon Anglo-French supplies. On the Turkish Front proper, the British invasion of Mesopotamia was just beginning; and in the fourth sphere of operations, the overseas colonies, minor actions were occurring against German colonial possessions.

The Western Front

January–March: Allied offensive in the Champagne and Artois area attempted to free French territory from German control, with limited effect as German counter-attacks stabilized the situation. British forces had a noted success at Neuve Chapelle (10 March), but bad coordination of support allowed the Germans to recover the lost ground.

6–15 April: French offensive at the Battle of the Woëvre beaten off.

22 April–25 May: Under cover of the first use in the West of poison gas, the German offensive of the 2nd Battle of Ypres temporarily broke the Allied line; but lack of support occasioned by the drain in manpower to the Eastern Front prevented a renewed drive, and after very heavy combat the British stabilized the line, having suffered enormous casualties.

May–June: Allied offensives made limited progress, the British drive being stopped near Festubert (May) and the French around Vimy Ridge (late May and June, also styled the 2nd Battle of Artois). After this both sides neared temporary exhaustion and merely held their positions.

September–November: Again the Allies took the offensive, having recouped their strength. A concerted attempt to break the German line had been planned by Joffre: in the 3rd Battle of Artois and 2nd Battle of Champagne the French made little progress; similarly the British at Loos (25 September–14 October). After further immense loss of life for little effect, the effort was abandoned, and in December Sir John French (taking the blame for lack of success) was replaced as British commander by Sir Douglas Haig, who held this command on the Western Front to the end of the war. Losses on the Western Front had been appalling beyond belief – almost 1.3 million French, over 600,000 Germans and 280,000 British – yet the battle lines on 31 December remained virtually as they had been on 1 January.

The Eastern Front

January: The efforts of the Central Powers were successful in the east, compared with the stalemate on the Western Front. The plan was to concert an attack on the Russian defenders of Poland from the Austrians in the south and the Germans in the north. On 31 January at Bolimov the Germans used poison gas for the first time, though with less success than later on the Western Front.

February: At the 2nd Battle of the Masurian Lakes, Hindenburg's Germans made considerable progress; but a Russian counter-attack (22 February) stabilized the position.

March: In Galicia the Russians successfully resisted Austrian attempts to relieve beleaguered Przemysl, which fell to the Russians on 22 March.

May–June: German resources were concentrated into reinforcing the Eastern Front, and an immense assault from 2 May burst through the Russian line, recapturing Przemysl (3 June).

June–December: As the Central Powers followed up their breakthrough, the Russians began a dogged retreat, only the skill of their commander, Grand Duke Nicholas, and the determination of the ordinary soldiers preventing a defeat of massive proportions. The onset of winter and the seasonal deterioration of the roads ended the 300-mile conquest, Vilna being captured by the Germans on 19 September. By then the Grand Duke had been removed (unfairly) and replaced by the Tsar in nominal command. The year ended with the Russians clinging to a front line virtually on the Russian frontier. The Central Powers had lost about a million men in the year's campaigning on the Eastern Front, and the Russians about the same, plus a further million captured.

The Caucasus

January: A Turkish attempt to advance north-east into the Russian Caucasus was repelled by a Russian victory at Sarikamish (3 January).

July: Russian failure to exploit Sarikamish allowed the Turks to resume their offensive, winning a victory near Van (16 July), but they retired upon the approach of Russian reinforcements.

August–December: Fighting continued without a decision; Grand Duke Nicholas was transferred from the Eastern Front from late September and began to prepare for a renewed offensive in 1916.

The Dardanelles

The Allied expedition to the Dardanelles was undertaken to relieve pressure on Russia and to remove Turkey from the war. The descent was an Anglo-French enterprise, initially a naval expedition, which was repelled by the Turkish defenders (18 March), and then by a military expedition under General Ian Hamilton, which was opposed by the German General Liman von Sanders.

25 April: Allied landings at Cape Helles and 15 miles farther north at Ari Burnu, the latter conducted by the ANZACs (Australian and New Zealand Army Corps). Neither landing was especially well-managed, and both met the stiffest opposition from Turkish forces in strong positions overlooking the landing beaches.

6–8 August: After a summer of bitter fighting around the landing areas, a strong British reinforcement landed at Suvla, north of Ari Burnu, to coincide with pushes from both the existing beachheads. Though Suvla successfully opened another field of operations, still little progress could be made against the resolute defenders.

August–December: Hamilton was replaced in mid-October, but the brutal fighting continued until the Allied commanders decided that the only practical move was to abandon the whole expedition; the evacuation was to be completed in January 1916. The Dardanelles expedition, though strategically valid, was one of the costliest failures of the war. Under the name 'Gallipoli' it became a synonym for extreme privation and untold feats of heroism on the part of both sides.

The Middle East

British efforts against the Turks were also made in the Middle East; in 1915 these were largely directed towards Mesopotamia. In January–February a Turkish attack against the Suez Canal was repelled by the British forces in Egypt; no further operations occurred on this front, but the threat was sufficient to prevent the British from releasing all the necessary resources to support the Dardanelles expedition.

January: British forces at Basra were built up to contemplate an advance on Baghdad, but initially Turkish probes had to be repelled. By midsummer about one-third of the distance to Baghdad had been covered by General Charles Townshend. In support, General G. F. Gorringe advanced up the Euphrates on Townshend's left and won a minor victory at Nasiriya (24 July).

September: Townshend continued to advance upon Kut-al-Amara, two-thirds of the way from Basra to Baghdad. The Turks were driven from Kut (27–28 September) and withdrew to Ctesiphon, midway from Kut to Baghdad; despite Townshend being in need of reinforcement, his superior, Sir John Nixon, ordered him to press on.

November: Townshend attacked Ctesiphon (22 November). After initial success, his lack of resources and Turkish reinforcements decided him to return to Kut (26 November), where he arrived on 3 December. Four days later he was besieged and in a parlous state.

In addition to the Anglo-Turkish conflict in Mesopotamia, sporadic fighting occurred throughout the year in Persia, which, though neutral itself, had been largely occupied by Russian forces. Russo–Turkish conflict there was subsidiary to the main spheres of operations in the Caucasus and Mesopotamia.

The Serbian Front

Serbia was important to the Central Powers if communication between Germany and Turkey were to be maintained; neutral Roumania closed the rail-link in June, which to a degree precipitated the main attack on Serbia, in which Germany and Austria were joined by Bulgaria. Bulgaria's entry into the war prompted Greece to mobilize in support of Serbia, and to aid the Greeks a Franco-British expedition was sent to Salonika (October); but immediately the pro-Allied Greek prime minister, Venizelos, was removed by the king, who declared Greek neutrality.

October: Serbia was overwhelmed by four enemy armies, one German, one Austrian and two Bulgarian. The Allies in Salonika were too weak to prevent the disaster.

November: With the Franco-British troops able only to defend Salonika, the Serbian Army retreated into Montenegro and Albania, from where the remnant was shipped to Corfu to be re-equipped and reorganized. The Allied intervention was uncoordinated and too weak to be of use, and was further embarrassed by being in possession of territory belonging to a neutral.

The Italian Front

A new front in Europe was opened when Italy joined the war on the side of the Allies (23 May) by a declaration of war on Austria (not Germany).

June–December: The Italians attempted to attack Austria on the Isonzo Front (north of Trieste). Four battles along the River Isonzo occurred (June/July, July/August, October/November and November/December), none of which actions enabled the Italians to make much progress against stout Austrian defence.

The situation at the end of 1915, despite the losses of immense numbers of men on both sides, was generally a stalemate. The Western Front remained static; Turkey had successfully repelled the Dardanelles expedition and limited British progress in Mesopotamia; while the Central Powers had achieved considerable success on the Eastern Front and in Serbia. Lack of Allied coordination had proved extremely costly and continued to inhibit the full utilization of their resources.

BRITISH ARMY SMALL ARMS (excluding machine-guns)

Until after the Boer War two varieties of personal firearm had been carried by the British Army: the infantry rifle and the cavalry carbine. The inefficiency of the latter having been proven in the Boer War, a universal rifle was intended for both dismounted and mounted troops (although a number of variants were actually carried). To accommodate both services, the existing infantry Lee-Enfield magazine rifle (approved in November 1895, although it did not immediately displace the variant of the first British magazine rifle, the Lee-Metford, currently in service) was reduced in length and styled the Short Magazine Lee-Enfield or SMLE (in several 'Marks'), 44½in overall (as against the 49½in of the earlier rifles, Lee-Enfield, Lee-Metford and Martini-Henry). It was introduced in 1902, and from 1905–7 a quantity of earlier Lee-Enfields and Lee-Metfords were converted to SMLE, and others modified to permit 'charger' loading of the magazine (by which five rounds could be inserted simultaneously, a system developed by Lee in 1892). The bolt-action rifle of .303in calibre weighed 8lb 10½oz without bayonet (1lb extra), and in the hands of a skilled infantryman (like those of the BEF of 1914) could discharge 15 rounds per minute and was capable of great accuracy. (Various Marks were in simultaneous use: for example, in their first action in 1914 the London Scottish found their Mark Is prone to jamming, so they exchanged them for improved Mark IIIs that were available on the battlefield).

In 1911–13 a new rifle of .276in calibre was developed, known as the 'Pattern 1913', of which a number were made for trial, but its adoption was prevented by the outbreak of war. Some of those produced were adapted to .303in and issued as snipers' rifles as they were capable of superior accuracy. The .303in calibre variant was styled 'Pattern 1914' (P.14) and from 1915 was manufactured for Britain in the United States by Winchester, Remington and Eddystone, and was used alongside the Lee-Enfield. From 1917, when the USA ran short of its own Springfield rifle, the P.14 was adapted to the US .300in calibre cartridge and issued to the US Army under the title 'Model 1917 (Enfield)'.

A number of older weapons were also used by British forces; even the single-shot Martini-Henry (developed in 1871–2 and originally issued in 1874, with improvements in 1876 and 1879) was used by some home-defence troops. The forces from the Dominions tended to use standard British weapons, though a distinctive pattern was used by the Canadian Army, the Mark III Ross rifle of 1910, also .303in and a development of the 1907 Mark II. It was an extremely accurate weapon but so prone to becoming fouled that by 1916 it was withdrawn and replaced by the Lee-Enfield, although some were retained for sniping.

The bayonet, long considered the British Army's 'traditional' weapon, remained important. The basic pattern in use was

bayonet in a hand-to-hand fight, was removed in 1913, although photographs of the First World War occasionally show it still in use. The P.14 was equipped with a bayonet not dissimilar, but the Ross had a shorter, sturdy blade akin to trench-knives, the privately-acquired weapons carried in considerable numbers especially in the later stages of the war (as were a variety of

styled a 'sword bayonet' having a single-edged, knife-shaped blade with deep fullers, wooden grip and steel quillon. The 1903 Lee-Enfield bayonet had been almost 15in long; probably to compensate for the reduction in length of the SMLE, the 1907—pattern was increased to a blade-length of 17in. The hooked quillon, designed initially to catch or throw off the enemy's

ORGANIZATIONAL TABLES: THE BRITISH ARMY

(Organization naturally varied with circumstances, but the following is a basic outline of the principal formations):

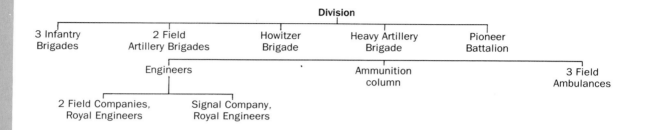

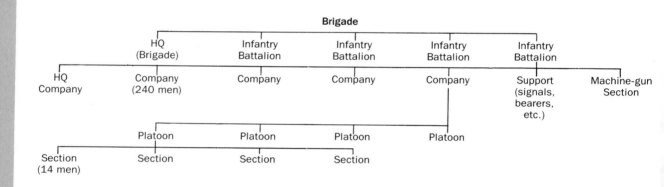

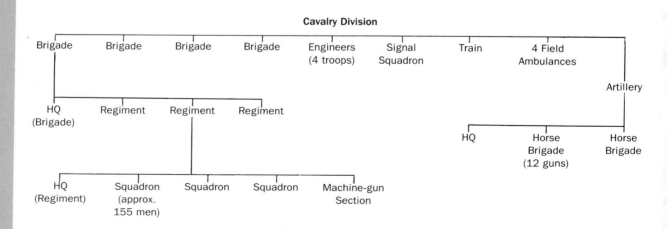

trench-clubs). The 1905-pattern Ross had a fine point, which was recognized as defective in action and was modified by grinding down the blade in 1907.

Swords were carried by officers and cavalry; the 1908-pattern cavalry sabre, which had a thin but strong blade designed for the thrust and a metal grip that provided an excellent hand-guard, was probably the finest cavalry weapon *ever* devised and compelled the user to execute the thrust, which the British Army had finally acknowledged as the most effective blow. Ironically, by the time this well-designed weapon was issued, the opportunities for its use in combat were virtually nil: in the only large-scale cavalry actions of the old style in the war, against the Turks, the sword had been virtually discarded and bayonets were used in its place. The swords of infantry officers existed in several patterns (officers of most Scottish regiments had the traditional Highland broadsword with basket hilt) but were rarely carried on active service.

Unlike the armies of some European nations, Britain preferred the revolver as a pistol rather than the automatic: the Webley Mark IV was typical: a 6-shot, .442in calibre weapon, double-action and self-extracting (the cartridges being ejected when the gun was 'broken' and the barrel depressed). The revolver was carried principally by officers and, like all pistols, was only of use at shorter ranges.

Hand-grenades were much neglected at the outbreak of war, only a few members of the Royal Engineers being trained to throw the 'No. 1' grenade, which consisted of a fragmentation-head mounted on a 16in cane with a 36in streamer to ensure that it landed nose-down, ignition being caused by the impact of landing. Patterns No. 2 (or 'Mexican', copied from an export order for that nation) and Nos. 3 (the Marten-Hale rifle-grenade) and similar 4 were all used prior to late 1915, but shortages led to the manufacture of grenades in the field, often from old tin cans (hence the colloquial name 'jam-tin bombs'). A wide variety of other patterns were devised, ranging from egg-shaped projectiles, some resembling the jam-tin, explosive devices on a wooden pallet resembling a hair-brush, archaic-looking cylindrical bombs resembling a Napoleonic howitzer-shell in miniature (No. 15), to a variety of rifle-grenades, some of dubious value and more dangerous to the thrower than the enemy. The best pattern was the No. 5, introduced in early 1915 and manufactured by the Mills Munition Company. It never completely replaced other patterns, but the 'Mills bomb' in its several guises became the commonest grenade in British

service, and also existed in a rifle-grenade version, although variations on the Marten-Hale were also developed. The later patterns no longer relied upon percussion ignition (i.e., the impact of landing) but had an internal mechanism that exploded the charge by a plunger released by the extraction of a pin before throwing.

BRITISH ARMY RANK MARKINGS

Rank-insignia for NCOs took the form of chevrons on the upper arm: lance-corporal (or equivalent), one; corporal, two; sergeant, three; company quartermaster-sergeant (and company sergeant-major to 1915), three with crown above; CSM after 1915 (and regimental sergeant-major before) crown on lower sleeve; regimental QMS, star over four inverted chevrons (from 1915 crown in wreath on lower sleeve); RSM after 1915, royal coat of arms on lower sleeve.

Officers' insignia were in the form of stars and crown on the shoulder-strap of the greatcoat and foreign service tunic, and on the cuff for ordinary service dress, a 'gauntlet' cuff for Highland regiments and a flapped cuff for others. Badges and braid were in light drab: 2nd lieutenant, star, one line of braid; lieutenant, 2 stars, 1 line; captain, 3 stars, 2 lines; major, crown, three lines; lieutenant-colonel, crown and star, three lines; colonel, crown and two stars, four lines.

BRITISH ARMY BATTALION-IDENTIFICATION

The great increase in the number of battalions fielded by a regiment, and the anonymity of the khaki service uniform, caused the introduction of battalion-identity signs in cloth at the back of the collar or, on the sleeve below the shoulder. That these seldom bore many common regimental devices is illustrated by the battalion-insignia illustrated here, of the Lancashire Fusiliers.

A: 'Ordinary' cuff, left to right: lieutenant; 2nd lieutenant.
B: 'Highland' cuff, left to right: lieutenant-colonel; major; captain.

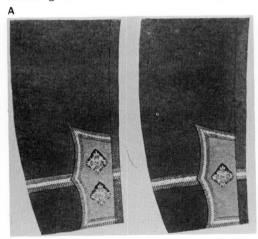

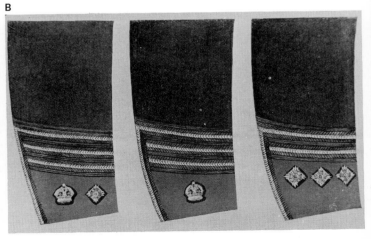

A

B

1st Bn: fig. 1, orange-yellow (left) and crimson.

2nd Bn: fig. 2, crimson with orange-yellow centre (sleeve).

1/5th Bn: fig. 3, red, bearing white '5' (sleeve).

2/5th Bn (formed Sept. 1914): fig. 4, red.

3/5th Bn (formed Oct. 1914): fig. 3, dark green (sleeve).

2/6th Bn (formed Sept. 1914): fig. 3, red (sleeve).

1/7th Bn: fig. 3, red, bearing white '7' (sleeve).

2/7th Bn (formed Aug. 1914): fig 3, yellow (sleeve).

1/8th Bn: fig. 3, red, bearing white '8' (sleeve).

2/8th Bn (formed Sept. 1914): fig. 3, black (sleeve).

9th Bn (formed Aug. 1914): fig. 5, yellow with black number (indicating 2nd bn of 34th Inf. Bde, 11th Div., from 1915).

10th Bn (formed Sept. 1914): each company had different sign. A Coy: fig. 6, crimson (left) and yellow; B Coy: fig 6, yellow (left) and crimson; C Coy: fig. 7, crimson (left) and yellow; D Coy: fig. 7, yellow (left) and crimson.

11th Bn (formed Sept. 1914): fig. 8, black bar over two red bars.

15th Bn (formed Sept. 1914): each company had different sign, all of fig. 9 with upper red triangle: HQ Coy with black bars, A

Coy red bars, B Coy dark green bars, C Coy yellow bars, D Coy blue bars.

16th Bn (formed Nov. 1914): each company had different sign, all of fig. 10 with upper red triangle, HQ Coy with red triangle alone; A–D Coys with three bars coloured as for 15th Bn.

17th Bn (formed Dec. 1914): fig 11, yellow (sleeve).

18th Bn (formed Jan. 1915): fig. 12, dark blue (sleeve). (On back of collar, two vertical dark blue bars, one over the other.)

19th Bn (formed Jan. 1915): fig. 13, red. (From Dec. 1917 a yellow rectangle upon crimson diamond worn at rear of greatcoat collar.)

20th Bn (formed March 1915): fig. 14, purple.

Such signs were normally worn only on active service; thus battalions like the 3/, 4/Lancashire Fusiliers, etc., which remained at home, had no such insignia. The 12th Bn. (65th Bde, 22nd Div.) and 23rd Bn (176th Bde, 59th Div; 121st Bde, 40th Div. from June 1918) wore only the sign of their respective divisions. A full table of this unit's signs is in *History of the Lancashire Fusiliers 1914–18* (J. C. Latter, Aldershot, 1949).

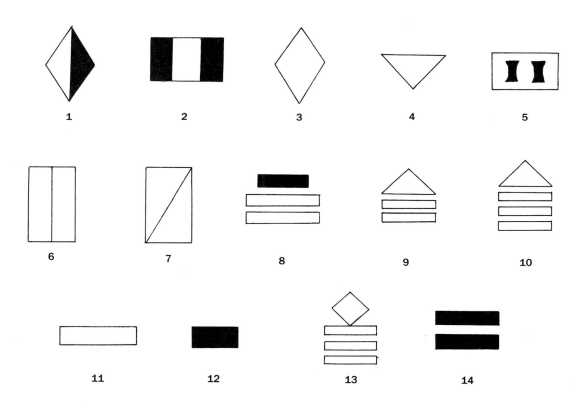

1   2   3   4   5

6   7   8   9   10

11   12   13   14

ORDER OF BATTLE: GALLIPOLI

The following skeleton order of battle lists the regiments involved: there were in addition the usual artillery and supporting services provided by New Zealand and Australia, and by the British Army with Indian Mountain Artillery for the Royal Naval Division; plus the Palestinian-Jewish Zion Mule Corps attached to ANZAC Headquarters.

I ANZAC Corps

HQ and troops attached at Corps level:

2nd Lt. Horse Bde: 5th (Queensland), 6th and 7th (NSW) Lt Horse

3rd Lt. Horse Bde: 8th (Victoria), 9th (Victoria/S. Australia) and 10th (W. Australia) Lt Horse

Ceylon Planters' Rifle Corps (attached to HQ)

1st Australian Div:

HQ etc: 4th (Victoria) Lt Horse
1st Australian Bde: 1st–4th NSW Btns
2nd Australian Bde: 5th–8th Victoria Btns
3rd Australian Bde: 9th Queensland, 10th S. Australia, 11th W.
 Australia, 12th S. Australia/W. Australia/Tasmania Btns
2nd Australian Div:
HQ etc: 13th (Victoria) Lt Horse
5th Australian Bde: 17th–20th NSW Btns
6th Australian Bde: 21st–24th Victoria Btns
7th Australian Bde: 25th Queensland, 26th Queensland/
 Tasmania, 27th S. Australia, 28th W. Australia Btns
New Zealand and Australian Div:
NZ Bde: Auckland, Canterbury, Otago and Wellington Btns
NZ Mounted Rifle Bde: Auckland, Canterbury and Wellington
 Mtd Rifles

4th Australian Bde: 13th NSW, 14th Victoria, 15th Queensland/
 Tasmania, 16th S. and W. Australia Btns
1st Australian Lt Horse Bde: 1st (NSW), 2nd (Queensland), 3rd
 (S. Australia/Tasmania) Lt Horse
29th Indian Bde: 14th Prince of Wales's Own Ferozepore Sikhs;
 1/5th, 1/6th and 2/10th Gurkha Rifles (Frontier Force)
Royal Naval Div:
Royal Marine Bde: Chatham and Portsmouth Btns, RM
1st Royal Naval Bde: Nelson Btn, RN, Deal Btn, RM

C and D: In 1915 the *Illustrated London News* captioned these photographs of a sergeant of a fusilier regiment wearing the 1908 web equipment.

C

D

Original British contingent:

29th Division:

86th Inf. Bde: 2/R. Fusiliers, 1/Lancashire Fusiliers, 1/R. Munster Fusiliers, 1/R. Dublin Fusiliers

87th Inf. Bde: 2/S. Wales Borderers, 1/King's Own Scottish Borderers, 1/R. Inniskilling Fusiliers, 1/Border Regt

88th Inf. Bde: 4/Worcestershire Regt, 2/Hampshire Regt, 1/Essex Regt, 5/R. Scots

SOURCES AND BIBLIOGRAPHY

This lists some works applicable to the war as a whole, as presented in the earlier title *1914*, but emphasis is here given to the campaigns of 1915 and to the British Army, which features in the data section. The literature is immense, and the following are either some of the most significant or the most easily-accessible for further reading.

Anon *The Anzac Book* (London, 1916) a celebration of the Anzacs and their campaign in the Dardanelles.

Barker, A. J. *The Neglected War: Mesopotamia 1914–18* (London, 1967).

Barnes, R. M. *The British Army of 1914* (London, 1968).

Chappell, M. *British Battle Insignia 1914–18* (London, 1986).

Chappell, M. *British Infantry Equipments 1908–80* (London, 1980).

Chappell, M. *The British Soldier in the 20th Century: Service Dress 1902–40* (Hatherleigh, 1987).

Chappell M. *The British Soldier in the 20th Century: Field Service Head-Dress* (Hatherleigh, 1987).

Denton, K. *Gallipoli: One Long Grave* (Sydney, 1986).

Fosten, D. S. V., and R. J. Marrion *The British Army 1914–18* (London, 1978).

Fosten, D. S. V., and R. J. Marrion *The German Army 1914–18* (London, 1978).

James, E. A. *British Regiments 1914–18* (London, 1978), a register of units and the formations in which they served.

Laffin, J. *Damn the Dardanelles* (London, 1980).

Mollo, A. *Army Uniforms of World War I* (Poole, 1977), the most comprehensive and valuable modern work on the subject.

Moorhead, A. *Gallipoli* (London, 1956).

Nash, D. B. *Imperial German Army Handbook 1914–18* (London, 1980).

Nash, D. B. *German Infantry 1914–18* (Edgeware, 1971).

Walter, A. (ed.) *Guns of the First World War* (London, 1988), a reprint of the *Text Book of Small Arms*, 1909.

Wilson, H. W. (ed.) *The Great War* (London, 1915), contemporary work that includes many significant photographs.

▼42

42. The advent of poison gas produced some of the most unearthly-looking soldiers in history, as exemplified by these French *poilus* wearing anti-gas hoods (an appearance compared by the *Illustrated War News* with that of the staff of the Spanish Inquisition!). They also wear khaki overall-coats apparently over the equipment (presumably an attempt at camouflage prior to the issue of 'horizon blue'), and carry the 1886 Lebel rifle (modified 1893), at 8mm calibre the first small-bore military rifle officially adopted. Its metal-hilted bayonet of cross-shaped section, with hooked quillon, is well illustrated here.

43. A platoon of British soldiers wearing a variety of anti-gas helmets. The first protection was nothing more than a pad worn over the nose and mouth, often with goggles; but these men wear a number of more elaborate masks, some with rectangular viewing-slits and others with transparent patches for the eyes. The small pouches worn around the neck or over the shoulder were the means of carrying the mask in a place accessible for immediate use.

44. Following the rudimentary face-pads adopted as anti-gas protection early in the war, the next common British style was this hood-like helmet made of blue-grey or khaki cloth, with metal-edged eye-holes and a leather valve at the mouth, a voluminous garment, which had to be tucked inside the tunic-collar. The helmets were appallingly uncomfortable (a metal tube connected to the valve had to be held between the teeth) and produced an inhuman appearance.

45. A French infantryman in trench-fighting kit showing the 1915 uniform. He wears the new 'horizon blue' greatcoat with breast-pockets and blue regimental number on the collar, the Adrian steel helmet and apparently only rudimentary gas-protection, a muffler and goggles. The weapons shown were ideal for combat in the close confines of a trench: a privately-acquired dagger and a revolver, which appears to be the French Model 1892 8mm weapon.

43 ▲ 44 ▼ 45 ▼

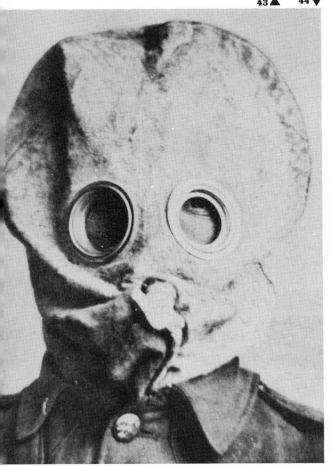

46. Only in late 1915 were the first British 'shrapnel helmets' issued to troops on active service. These were of the pressed-steel pattern known as a 'Brodie' (after its designer) and resembled a medieval *chapelle de fer* or a bowler hat, hence its nickname 'battle bowler'. (A more universal pseudonym was the ubiquitous 'tin hat'.) This group of officers, photographed in late 1915, wear winter trench equipment including the goatskin 'teddy bear' jerkins originally used in the winter of 1914–15. It was common at this period for officers to purchase helmets privately from their outfitters, some of which were slightly different from the regulation pattern.

47. 'Over the top': a British charge in the Dardanelles. A number of photographs purporting to be action scenes from Gallipoli were in fact taken during training for the actual landings (French troops being also depicted in such photographs), but many genuine Gallipoli scenes were photographed *in situ*. The men depicted here are members of the Royal Naval Division that accompanied the ANZAC landings, wearing field equipment (less knapsack) and the tropical-service topee.

48. The Turkish Army adopted a khaki service dress from 1909, their equipment influenced by German styles, though unique was the khaki cloth 'Enver-Pasha' helmet shown here. Officers and mounted troops might wear instead a grey or black *kalpak* or lambskin busby. Equipment was brown leather, and officers wore knee-boots instead of the khaki puttees of the rank-and-file. Arm-of-service colours (worn on the collar) were khaki (infantry), olive-green (rifles or light infantry), dark blue (artillery), light grey (cavalry), light blue (engineers), red (train), scarlet (general officers) and crimson (staff officers). Turkey adopted the 7.65mm Mauser rifle in 1890; the national patterns of Mauser varied in detail, the Turkish version having the same calibre

▲46 ▼47

as the Belgian but with similarities to the Spanish pattern.

49. Turkey's army was re-modelled with German guidance shortly before the war and comprised two basic categories: 25 *Nizam* or regular divisions (each of 13 infantry battalions, 24 guns and a cavalry squadron) and a similar number of *Redif* or reserve divisions, one division of each combining to form a corps; but only the *Nizam* divisions were really effective, and benefitted much from German advice. Among the Turkish troops were those from the Arab territories; these infantrymen wear the Turkish service uniform but with native headdress and carry German drums. The drummers' shoulder-decorations are in Turkish style, but closely resemble the drummers' 'wings' used by the German Army.

48 ▲ 49 ▼

50 ▼

50. 'Digger': an anonymous Australian representing the magnificent ANZAC troops who served with extreme heroism in the Dardanelles, Europe and the Middle East. Their equipment was basically of British style, the tunic (originally of khaki flannel which faded to grey/blue, and later of khaki serge) was of an individual style, with voluminous pockets and plain buttons. The badge worn on the upturned brim of the slouch hat and on the point of the collar comprised a crown upon a 'rising sun' device, supposedly inspired by a wall-decoration of a 'fan' of bayonets. The brass shoulder-title 'AUSTRALIA' was universal. The battalion-identification badge on the sleeve is the upright rectangle of the 5th Australian Division, perhaps the brown and red of the 55th Battalion.

▲51   ▼52

51. Australian recruits about to embark for active service, Queenslanders according to the caption on the original: 'I am going to the Front with the Queensland . . . I Bade Chas. & Mrs. N. good bye . . . dont faint when you see this . . .'. Note the Australian tunic with its voluminous pockets; the web equipment is the British 1908 pattern. The oldest recruit at the extreme left appears to wear Boer War medal-ribbons.

52. A 'carrying party' at Gallipoli, exhibiting the first modifications of costume which soon multiplied until the ANZACS were nicknamed 'the naked Australians'. These men retain their ordinary service uniform, in some cases with the neck unfastened (as permitted officially for the march in Europe), and wear the 1908-pattern web equipment, the leading man having unfastened his waist-belt and removed his puttees. The caps are the variety with ear-flaps designed to protect from the cold, needed in the Dardanelles winter.

53. Australians at Gallipoli engaged in a most unpleasant task, which concerned the combatants of all nations: attempting to rid shirts and underclothing of lice. Attempts to eradicate vermin varied from fumigation (where possible) to the application of patent poisons or even to applying candle-wax to the internal seams of garments, but none was completely successful and often the only temporary relief was to crush the lice manually along the seams where they most commonly resided.

54. Probably no piece of military equipment of the war was as famous as the French '75', the 75mm field-gun introduced in 1894. The classic *Soixante-Quinze* was the Model 1897 gun, and it performed sterling service throughout the war. Its major development was in the first truly effective control of recoil. This example is part of a battery dug in at the Dardanelles and

protected by a rudimentary breastwork; immediately beside the gun is its limber, with harness-pole detached, and upturned so that its open top faced the gunners, who were thus able to extract shells without having to reach up. The circular bases of the shells face the gunners in this illustration, and a pile of empty shell-cases is stacked at the rear. Most of the gunners have the French tropical helmet worn in the Dardanelles campaign.

53 ▲

54 ▼

▲55   ▼56

▼57

55. Dispatch-riders of the Royal Engineers at Gallipoli, with transport-vessels in the background. This depicts a typical assortment of Gallipoli uniforms, ranging from shirt-sleeves to vest and singlets, caps with neck-curtains, topees and Australian slouch hats. Motorcycles were useful for carrying messages even in such comparatively confined spaces as the landing-grounds of the Dardanelles, but horses were also used.

56. 'Annie' in action at Gallipoli: a British heavy battery bombarding Turkish positions. ('Annie' is the name painted on the barrel of the gun.) The crew wear typical Gallipoli dress: shirt-sleeves, shorts and caps with neck-cloths. The rather casual attitude of the men working on the hazardous fuzed nosecaps of shells in the foreground recalls the caption to the Bairnsfather cartoon of advice given to a man attempting to remove a nosecap with a hammer and chisel: 'Give it a good hard 'un; you can generally hear them fizzing if they are going to explode!'

57. Manufacturing hand-grenades at Gallipoli. The dearth of proper grenades led to the utilization (both on the Western Front and in the Dardanelles) of home-made missiles constructed of empty food-containers and hence the name 'jam-tin bombs': tin cans filled with explosive and improvised shrapnel. These British or Australian troops (note the slouch hat worn by the figure at far right) are producing such grenades and cutting fragments of barbed wire to pack with the explosive to produce weapons capable of causing terrible injury. The two men at the right are chopping up strands of barbed wire upon an anvil.

58. Gallipoli: captured Turks are interrogated by British staff officers. The two British soldiers who guard the prisoners (left) apparently wear caps with ear-flaps fastened over the crown, and one at least wears shorts and puttees. The two officers questioning the Turks wear the

ordinary uniform with rank-marking on the sleeve; but the pipe-smoking officer at the right has his rank-insignia on the shoulder-straps of the tunic. The officer in the cap apparently has a white neck-curtain attached (khaki was the usual colour), and the other wears a staff brassard (commonly called an 'armlet') on the left arm, an item which came into considerable use during the war as a means of identifying the wearer's function or even the unit to which he was attached, when the formation's distinctive sign might be stitched to the brassard.

59. A wounded Turkish prisoner accepts a drink from the canteen of a member of the British landing force at Gallipoli. The British uniform includes the cap with ear-flaps fastened up over the crown, shorts (conceivably produced by cutting off the lower leg of the trousers, a common practice), and puttees over bare lower legs. The bayonet retains its curved quillon, generally removed in 1913 but still in evidence in a number of photographs dating from the earlier years of the war.

▲60

60. An unusual item of equipment deployed in a trench at 'Anzac' (the Gallipoli landing): a French spray designed to counteract the effect of poison gas. A contemporary recipe for

▼62

this liquid described its composition as 800 grammes of water to 200 grammes of carbonate of soda crystals, 1,000 grammes of hyposulphate of soda and 150 grammes of glycerine.

▲61

The man carrying the canister wears typical Gallipoli dress: a cap with neck-guard, vest and trousers. The officer in the background retains a more conventional uniform.

61. An ANZAC sniping-party at Gallipoli. These Australians wear typical Gallipoli uniform: shirt or vest, shorts and puttees or socks, and equipment reduced to a minimum. The sniper here operates a rifle sighted through a periscope, enabling him to fire over the sandbag parapet without showing himself; his 'observer' views through another periscope, while the other men – probably 'escorts' in case of a sudden raid by the Turks – sit with an air of resignation until something occurs. All wear the Australian slouch hat save for the sniper himself, who appears to wear an empty sandbag on his head, camouflage in case he should accidentally move into view over the top of the parapet.

62. The evolution of the ANZAC 'Gallipoli' uniform was a progressive degeneration from the regulation dress in an attempt to combat the appallingly arduous climate. From shirt-sleeves the 'uniform' in hot weather was reduced to vests, and then often only to shorts, boots, socks and slouch

hat – hence the sobriquet 'the naked Australians'. The 'shorts' were originally nothing more than the trousers hacked off at the knee or above, with no attempt to conceal or turn over the ragged edges of the cloth. These two ANZACs stand guard over a 'jack-in-the-green' figure, a captured Turkish sniper who still wears his foliage camouflage: 'sniping' was as great a hazard in the Dardanelles campaign as it became on the Western Front.

63. The increase in the use of the hand-grenade as a close-quarter weapon resulted in the devising of a number of new items of equipment, such as the bomb-carrying harness worn by this British fusilier at Salonika. It is difficult to determine which pattern of grenade is held here because of its concealment by the bomber's hand, but it *may* be the egg-shaped 'No 16' grenade. The single chevron visible on the left upper arm denotes the rank of lance-corporal.

64. In late 1915 the Serbian Army, having attempted to defend its country against overwhelming odds, was evacuated to Corfu for re-equipment in basically French style. These soldiers wear the native Serbian uniform of grey-green, which began to be introduced from 1912; however, it never reached the reserves and was worn only by the 'first Ban' or regulars. Arm-of-service was indicated by the facing-colour on the tunic and large patches on the greatcoat collar – crimson for the infantry illustrated here. Note the low boots of native style worn by the Serbian Army.

63 ▲   64 ▼

▲65

65. Much of Serbia's military and artillery transport was dragged by oxen (such unorthodox teams even being used by British gunners in Serbia), but these men have a better conveyance on the Salonika–Nish railway. The gunners wear the standard Serbian uniform with the black collar-patch of the artillery and the rather distinctively shaped grey-green cloth forage cap. Note that even in this theatre of operations the usual text is painted on the boxcar in the background: '40 men or 6 horses'.

66. The Bulgarian Army had begun to be re-equipped in grey-green Austrian-style uniform from 1908, but at her entry into the war this was not universal and older brown uniform and German stocks were pressed into service. The arm-of-service colour was carried on the collar-patch – here the infantry's crimson – and though the trousers were usually the same colour as the tunic, shortage of stocks probably resulted in a mixture of styles. The Russian-style cap was in the uniform-colour with black or grey-green leather peak; that illustrated lacks the usual oval cockade in the red/white/green national colours. Puttees or boots and gaiters were the prescribed wear, but this man demonstrates the usual shortages and wears civilian-style leggings and native hide sandals or *palanka*.

▼66

▼67

68 ▲

69 ▲

67. The Italian Army began the war in a mixture of the grey-green service uniform introduced in 1909 and older dark blue uniforms. The 1909 pattern illustrated included a loose tunic without pockets, with padded 'rolls' on the shoulders to hold the equipment in place, trousers and puttees, and boots with a high ankle. Regimental insignia was carried on the collar (patches of different colour and shape) and as a coloured (later black) embroidered or metal badge on the grey-green cloth kepi, which for other ranks was unstiffened until 1916. Equipment was black leather. The rifle was the 1891

Mannlicher Carcano, of 6.5mm calibre, and the older Vetterli rifle (of same calibre) was also used. The rifle had a knife-bayonet in a scabbard; the shorter Mannlicher Carcano carbine of 1891, however, had a triangularly-sectioned blade permanently attached, folding under the barrel when not in use.

68. This infantryman with an immense burden shows the rear of the Italian equipment, in this case not very symmetrically-arranged, including an untidily-folded grey-green greatcoat and spare boots carried atop the knapsack. The double-breasted

greatcoat had a deep falling collar; other garments included a fur-collared and cuffed grey-green knee-length winter coat; and a wrist-length cape of the same colour, with falling collar. Attached to the rear of the haversack below waist-level is the canteen; the mess-tin in its cover is strapped to the rear of the knapsack.

69. Italian officers wore a uniform similar to that of the other ranks, but with shoulder-straps and breast-pockets on the tunic. Being made of a lighter grey, these were easily distinguished by snipers; the other ranks' colour was generally

adopted where possible. The officers' kepi was stiffened and, unlike those of the rank and file, had a black leather peak instead of grey-green cloth. Rank-marking was borne upon the shoulder-straps (later transferred to the cuff) and kepi; the officer illustrated wears a single metal lace band around the kepi, which later in the war was replaced by less-obtrusive yellow or grey lace. He has the pointed-ended collar-patch of the line infantry, and puttees in place of the optional black knee-boots. Equipment was generally of grey-green leather, although brown was also used.

▲70 ▼71

72 ▲

73 ▲

70. A sergeant of Italian artillery about to fire a small mountain fieldpiece. Such weapons were used in the Italian colonial campaigns (in North Africa) but were equally suited to mountain warfare in Europe. The sergeant wears his rank-chevrons (gold for artillery) on the forearm, two narrow bands above one broad; his black collar-patch (the artillery colour) was pointed at the end farthest from the opening of the collar. The tropical helmet (with badges worn even on active service) was a variation on the home-service uniform.

71. A considerable part of the Italian Army's campaigning was conducted in mountainous terrain; here is a front-line outpost of a shallow trench, overlooking Austrian-held territory. The troops are easily-recognizable by their distinctive headdress as *Bersaglieri* or rifle corps, whose black 'round hats' had grey covers on service. Their famous black cock-feather plumes were worn on the tropical helmet, and even on the steel helmet when Italy adopted the Adrian pattern. Their collar-patch was crimson. Other Italian troops with a distinctive headdress were the *Alpini* (mountain troops), who wore a 'Robin Hood'-style hat with feather.

72. In a war that saw the reintroduction of such medieval features as steel helmets, the most anachronistic equipment of all was that of the Italian 'Death Companies'. Before Italy entered the war, volunteer detachments were formed for hazardous duty such as wire-cutting, and these troops were issued with iron helmets, armoured cuirasses, shoulder- and abdominal-protection, gauntlets and 'pikes' with wire-cutting heads. These 'Death Volunteers' were later given the title *militare ardiot* ('bold soldier') and in 1917 were organized into assault units of *Arditi*. The man illustrated here wears the three cuff-stars of captain's rank and carries a rifle in place of the wire-cutting 'pike'.

73. The device illustrated here was described by its contemporary caption as an example of 'vitriolic warfare', a canister of acid which sprayed its lethal fluid from the Austrian lines into the Italian trenches on the Isonzo Front. The crew appear to wear the new Austrian field-grey uniform adopted in 1915, similar to that in use before but with a turndown collar, and with field-grey puttees instead of the earlier trousers with integral gaiters.

▲74 ▼75

▼76

74. British operations in Mesopotamia were organized by the Indian Army, a delegation of responsibility that led to lack of coordination in this theatre. Like British infantry regiments, each Indian unit possessed a machine-gun section, armed initially with Maxims; this section prepares to open fire on a Mesopotamian hillside. The British officer wears usual campaign costume including shorts, topee and a cravat at the open neck of his tunic. In the left background is one of the transport-mules used to convey both Maxim and ammunition.

75. German troops destroying a railway-line in South-West Africa. The troops formed for the German African colonies wore a uniform of similar style to that used in Europe, but in khaki-yellow drill known as 'sand grey', with Swedish cuffs and facing-colours of cornflower blue for South-West Africa, poppy-red for the Cameroons and Togoland and white for East Africa, worn with the ordinary arm-of-service piping. In 1913 the uniform-colour was officially changed to field-grey, but sand-grey remained in use for some time. The headdress was a low, grey felt slouch hat edged with the colony facing-colour, and bore the national cockade on the upturned right brim; weapons and equipment were as used in Europe.

76. The surrender of German forces in South-West Africa on 9 July 1915 on the railway between Otavi and Khorab; General Botha (right) represents the Anglo–South African forces. Next to Botha, the German governor of the province, Dr Seitz, signs the document of surrender; at the left is Lieutenant-Colonel Francke, commander of the German forces. This illustrates to good effect the tropical uniform of the German troops; especially evident is the red, white and black cockade worn upon the upturned brim of the grey slouch hat, edged with cornflower blue.

77. Among the Germans' most effective opponents in East Africa were the King's African Rifles, a force formed in 1902 by the amalgamation of the Central Africa, Uganda and East Africa

78 ▲

Rifles, which were recruited from the 'martial races' of central Africa and the Sudan, with officers seconded from the British Army. Full dress consisted of khaki drill and fez, but the khaki service dress with blue puttees is shown here, worn by members of the 3rd (East Africa) Battalion. The light straps across the breast are those of the haversack and canteen; at the right hip was carried a native machete, and two rolls on the back, a blanket over a greatcoat. The pillbox caps have a rolled-up neck-curtain and bear the battalion designation ('III') on the front; officers wore similar caps but peaked, like a kepi. Sandals are shown here, but the

troops often preferred to go barefoot.

78. Although of comparatively minor significance, operations in East Africa absorbed considerable resources. The rail link between Nairobi and the coast was believed to be vulnerable to German raids, so the Uganda railway was provided with protection. Illustrated here is a 'mobile blockhouse': HMAT (His Majesty's Armoured Train) *Simba*, similar to the armoured, loopholed carriages used in South Africa during the great Boer War. A British officer with kit and bearer raises his topee to the photographer!

79. The Germans defended their African territory with considerable resolution, both sides using native units. This illustration shows a light fieldpiece in action at Jabassi in the Cameroons, directed by a British officer who appears to have a sun-shade draped over the front of his topee and secured under the upper vent. When this illustration was published in the *Illustrated War News* in September 1915, its caption made much of the heroism of the British West African Frontier Force, recounting an incident in which two natives had volunteered to act as the support for a machine-gun after its mounting had been shot away!

79 ▼

77 ▼

▲80

80. Co-operation between the component armies of the Central Powers was not always completely cordial, but this combined column of Austrian (left) and German infantry

▼81

(right) on the Eastern Front seems to comprise the 'brothers in arms' described by a contemporary caption. It is interesting to note the Austrian at the left front of his column,

who appears to wear the long woollen stockings of the mountain troops and *Landesschützen* in place of the ordinary Austrian legwear of trousers combined with anklet;

note also the prominent collar-patches on the Austrian greatcoats.

81. Austrian infantry crossing a river during the campaigning in

Galicia. As the Russians retired they destroyed many of the bridges, necessitating the use by the pursuing Central Powers of pontoons – in this case a 'flying bridge', a pontoon used as a punt, poled across the river. The infantry in the foreground wear the ordinary pike-grey field uniform (which in 1915 began to be replaced by a field-grey version, cut slightly looser), with the soft, pike-grey cap; but they appear to have a mixture of equipment. Some have the standard hide knapsack and brown leather belts, with the grey greatcoat rolled over the top of the knapsack; others appear to carry instead the rucksack of the *Landesschützen*.

82. Austrian cavalrymen captured in Galicia, with their Russian escort (extreme left and right). The Austrian uniforms represent one of the final uses of 'coloured' uniforms in action: a light blue tunic with red facings, red breeches, and a pelisse-like, fur-lined over-jacket styled a *Pelz*. Their head-dress varies from the black shako of the hussars, and the *czapka* of the *Uhlans* (lancers) with a grey or grey-blue cloth cover (figure

third from right), to the much more popular red cloth forage-cap bearing two buttons on the front and a cockade above. The Russians wear their standard grey-brown, voluminous greatcoats and peaked cloth cap.

83. The Austrian forces included their regular armies (Austrian and Hungarian) and the reserve army of *Landwehr*. These were not auxiliaries or militia but generally of a similar standard to the regulars; indeed, the *Landwehr* mountain troops (*Landesschützen*) were among the élite units of the army. From 1887 there was also a home-defence force of *Landsturm*, which, unlike the *Landwehr* which was generally uniformed like the regulars, wore less regulation items. Both the *Landsturm* of Austria and Germany made use of the peaked cap with black oilskin top, remarkably akin to the headdress worn by similar units in the 'War of Liberation' a century before. With their greatcoats and blanket-bandoliers, these *Landsturm* men manning a trench in Russian Poland uncannily resemble their forebears of 1814.

84. A German ski-borne patrol on the Eastern Front, showing the adaptation of the ordinary uniform according to conditions of climate and terrain. Four Bavarian ski battalions were formed in early 1915 and later grouped into the 3rd *Jägers*, serving in the Carpathians. They wore a hooded camouflage jacket and trousers of thin white fabric, over the ordinary uniform. This depicts the utilization of crossed ski-poles as a rest for the rifle. In addition to the ski battalions, others received white greatcoats and hoods for use in snowy conditions.

▲84

85. The Tsar's magnificent staff-car in Galicia. This group of Russian staff officers includes Tsar Nicholas II himself (third from left, with back to the open door of the car); the governor of Galicia (saluting him); Grand Duke Nicholas (far right), then commanding the Russian forces; and General Yanuchkevitch, chief of the general staff (standing in the car, second right). Later in the year,

▼85

following Russian reverses on the Eastern Front, the capable Grand Duke Nicholas was transferred to the Caucasus theatre and the Tsar himself took over in nominal command of the Russian forces on the Eastern Front.

86. This photograph was published in the British magazine *The Sphere* as having been taken by their own special

correspondent attached to the Russian Army in Poland, and it was stated that the gun was in action immediately before and after the photograph was taken. It presents a superb study of the 1910 Maxim gun used by the Russian Army, 7.62mm calibre, raised upon its bipod mounting, which folded back alongside the 'trail' upon which the gunner sits. The water-cooled gun was fed by a belt passing over the

'spool' at the right-hand edge of the shield, the gunner sighting through the small vertical slot in the shield.

87 ▲

87. The mode of transporting the Russian wheeled Maxim gun – dragged by ropes attached to towing bars – is illustrated in this view of Russian prisoners under German escort. The Russians wear typical service uniform, including the ubiquitous roll worn bandolier-fashion. When the British magazine *Illustrated War News* published this photograph in July 1915 it was accompanied by the caption 'An unsportsmanlike indignity inflicted on brave foes', i.e., being forced to drag their own guns. The concept that war should be 'sporting' would not have been recognized by those actually engaged in the fighting!

88. Despite its depressing view of the fate of an ally, this photograph was published in Britain as a genuine scene from the war, showing Russian infantry lying dead upon German barbed wire. Wire like this protected the trench-systems of all armies and added yet one more horror to the catalogue; it gave an awful truth to the British popular song that recounted the fate of a battalion hanging on the 'old barbed wire'.

86 ▼

88 ▼

The *Fotofax* series

A new range of pictorial studies of military subjects for the modeller, historian and enthusiast. Each title features a carefully-selected set of photographs plus a data section of facts and figures on the topic covered. With line drawings and detailed captioning, every volume represents a succinct and valuable study of the subject. New and forthcoming titles:

Warbirds
F-111 Aardvark
P-47 Thunderbolt
B-52 Stratofortress
Stuka!
Jaguar
US Strategic Air Power:
  Europe 1942–1945
Dornier Bombers
RAF in Germany

Vintage Aircraft
German Naval Air Service
Sopwith Camel
Fleet Air Arm, 1920–1939
German Bombers of WWI

Soldiers
World War One: 1914
World War One: 1915
World War One: 1916
Union Forces of the American
  Civil War
Confederate Forces of the
  American Civil War
Luftwaffe Uniforms
British Battledress 1945–1967
  (2 vols)

Warships
Japanese Battleships, 1897–
  1945
Escort Carriers of World War
  Two
German Battleships, 1897–
  1945
Soviet Navy at War, 1941–1945
US Navy in World War Two,
  1943–1944
US Navy, 1946–1980 (2 vols)
British Submarines of World
  War One

Military Vehicles
The Chieftain Tank
Soviet Mechanized Firepower
  Today
British Armoured Cars since
  1945
NATO Armoured Fighting
  Vehicles
The Road to Berlin
NATO Support Vehicles

The *Illustrated* series

The internationally successful range of photo albums devoted to current, recent and historic topics, compiled by leading authors and representing the best means of obtaining your own photo archive.

Warbirds
US Spyplanes
USAF Today
Strategic Bombers, 1945–1985
Air War over Germany
Mirage
US Naval and Marine Aircraft
  Today
USAAF in World War Two
B-17 Flying Fortress
Tornado
Junkers Bombers of World War
  Two
Argentine Air Forces in the
  Falklands Conflict
F-4 Phantom Vol II
Army Gunships in Vietnam
Soviet Air Power Today
F-105 Thunderchief
Fifty Classic Warbirds
Canberra and B-57
German Jets of World War Two

Vintage Warbirds
The Royal Flying Corps in
  World War One
German Army Air Service in
  World War One
RAF between the Wars
The Bristol Fighter
Fokker Fighters of World War
  One
Air War over Britain, 1914–
  1918
Nieuport Aircraft of World War
  One

Tanks
Israeli Tanks and Combat
  Vehicles
Operation Barbarossa
Afrika Korps
Self-Propelled Howitzers
British Army Combat Vehicles
  1945 to the Present
The Churchill Tank
US Mechanized Firepower
  Today
Hitler's Panzers
Panzer Armee Afrika
US Marine Tanks in World War
  Two

Warships
The Royal Navy in 1980s
The US Navy Today
NATO Navies of the 1980s
British Destroyers in World
  War Two
Nuclear Powered Submarines
Soviet Navy Today
British Destroyers in World
  War One
The World's Aircraft Carriers,
  1914–1945
The Russian Convoys, 1941–
  1945
The US Navy in World War
  Two
British Submarines in World
  War Two
British Cruisers in World War
  One
U-Boats of World War Two
Malta Convoys, 1940–1943

Uniforms
US Special Forces of World
  War Two
US Special Forces 1945 to the
  Present
The British Army in Northern
  Ireland
Israeli Defence Forces, 1948 to
  the Present
British Special Forces, 1945 to
  Present
US Army Uniforms Europe,
  1944–1945
The French Foreign Legion
Modern American Soldier
Israeli Elite Units
US Airborne Forces of World
  War Two
The Boer War
The Commandos World War
  Two to the Present
Victorian Colonial Wars

A catalogue listing these series and other Arms & Armour Press titles is available on request from: Sales Department, Arms & Armour Press, Artillery House, Artillery Row, London SW1P 1RT.